The Mega SCIENCE QUIZ

Berty Ashley is a molecular biologist with the Dystrophy Annihilation Research Trust. He works with rare genetic disorders. What is not rare, though, is to see him conducting quizzes or attending them. He is the author of the popular 'Easy Like Sunday Morning' series of quizzes published in *The Hindu*'s *Sunday Magazine*. He was the senior content editor for two seasons of the Tamil edition of 'Kaun Banega Crorepati'. He is also a lover of music— not only playing but collecting, as is evident by his growing stack of vinyl records of jazz, prog, Hindustani and heavy metal music. He and his partner, Akhila, live in Bengaluru, surrounded by books, music and an assortment of pens and guitars.

Akhila Phadnis is a freelance translator. She holds a master's in Translation Studies from Durham University, the UK, and in Psychology from Madras University, Chennai, Tamil Nadu. She enjoys reading, practising calligraphy, learning new languages, quizzing, playing board games and taking long walks by the beach.

The Mega
SCIENCE
QUIZ

BERTY ASHLEY
AND
AKHILA PHADNIS

RUPA

Published by
Rupa Publications India Pvt. Ltd 2019
7/16, Ansari Road, Daryaganj
New Delhi 110002

Sales centres:
Allahabad Bengaluru Chennai
Hyderabad Jaipur Kathmandu
Kolkata Mumbai

ISBN: 978-93-5333-710-0

First impression 2019

10 9 8 7 6 5 4 3 2 1

The moral right of the authors has been asserted.

Printed at HT Media Ltd, Gr. Noida

CONTENTS

INTRODUCTION

Science is a way of thinking much more than it is a body of knowledge.

—Carl Sagan

In a world that is slanting towards falsehoods and un-verifiable facts, science has stood the test of time to be that one pillar of truth that you can depend on. The ability to conduct experiments, collect empirical evidence, observe reactions, analyze data, and more, are processes that lead to a better, more in-depth understanding of life on Earth. Humans capable of communicating have existed on this planet for more than two hundred thousand years. But only within the last five thousand has mankind really blossomed into this highly developed civilization we are now. It is not hyperbole to say that science has paved the way for that. We, as a myriad group of people with different cultures and histories, all came together for one thing only—for science, the pursuit of the truth. From the first human in Africa who came up with a way to create fire to the lady in a lab in Bengaluru today who is working on modifying the DNA of bacteria according to her will, science has come a long way. Every generation leaves behind information which subsequent generations build on, to develop an inherently better world for the future. As Bernard of Chartres famously said in the twelfth century, *'nanos gigantum humeris insidentes'*—which Isaac Newton translated in 1675 as 'If I have seen further it is by standing on the shoulders of giants'—we are where we are only because of the hard work and scientific temperament shown by our ancestors.

Science has a way of either opening your mind to things you never knew, or offering answers and resolving questions you've always had. Either way, science changes your life for the better.

This is not a textbook, neither is it an encyclopaedia. It is a quiz book through which we hope to inspire you and those you share these facts with (or buy a copy of the book for), to actively go in search of answers, reach out and look for facts.

When India was looking for a national motto, they found it in the ancient *Mundaka Upanishad*. From 1950 onwards, India's motto has been '*Satyameva Jayate*' (Truth alone triumphs). As we progress into a fast-changing world, we are in an unfortunate situation where, as much as science and technology have evolved, there are certain individuals and groups of people bent on destroying data and twisting facts mostly for selfish purposes of monetary gain. If we are to take on this challenge, we need the upcoming generation to not just study science, but embrace it. What we set out to do with this book is to give you facts, trivia and funda that will make you enjoy science, and not think of it as some boring subject from school. We want to prove that regardless of what your profession is, or how old you are, you can always be interested in science. We hope that on every page, you find at least one thing that excites you—one new fact that makes you want to share it with someone else. Some small tidbit you want to tweet about, saying 'Today I Learnt (TIL)'.

Science is a force to be reckoned with. We wish you happy quizzing, and may the force be with you.*

---

*Some of the questions in this book first appeared in *The Hindu*'s *Sunday Magazine* quiz called 'Easy Like Sunday Morning'.

1. BAFFLING BIOLOGY

1. In 1976, evolutionary biologist Richard Dawkins coined this term for a self-replicating unit of information that follows evolutionary principles and leads to the spread of ideas, knowledge and cultural phenomena. This 'unit' has in recent times gone viral on social media, with it being used as a source of news and facts. What name did Dawkins give this unit of information?

2. This little organ was initially of great importance to doctors because they believed it was responsible for black bile, one of the four fluids once believed to govern human behaviour and health. However, subsequent discoveries about illnesses and their causes led to people neglecting this organ and it would often be removed in case of injury, as doctors thought it served no function. In the second half of the twentieth century, however, doctors realized that it plays an important role in filtering blood. Blood flows more slowly through this organ, allowing bacteria to be recognized and destroyed by our body's immune

mechanisms. This organ is essential in foetuses, as it produces red blood cells! Most fascinatingly of all— if injured, tiny fragments of this organ can spread to blood-rich areas and regenerate into new versions. One in five people may have more than one of this organ in them! What is this fabulous organ?

3. Plants possess a powerful agent that can help them heal wounds. This agent stimulates cell division, causing a protective layer to form and then heal the damaged tissue. What interesting name was this acid given, since it is a derivative of another similar hormone produced in painful situations in plants?

4. Despite the horror stories, poor little vampire bats almost never suck on humans (though Brazil has had an increase in bird-targeting bats inexplicably trying human blood recently). Depending on the species, the bats target domesticated animals or birds, and suck on their blood. They do this by releasing an anticoagulant into the blood to allow it to flow freely instead of clotting. What is the rather appropriate name given to this anticoagulating agent, considering the name of these bats?

5. Movement is associated with life. Plants do not move but there are proteins, m-RNA etc. inside their cells which do. This molecular movement is a necessary condition for life. There are certain entities, 'X', that do not show any molecular movement in their structure when they are independent. This has led to them being

described as 'organisms on the verge of life'. What are these entities, which are responsible for many losses of life and economy?

6. Early in the nineteenth century, hatmakers used an orange-coloured solution of Mercuric Nitrate to smoothen the leather, to make the felts required for the hats. A slow reaction released volatile free mercury, which poisoned the hatmakers and caused a disease called Erethism. This first turned their hair orange and then caused insanity. What character in children's literature is based on this true issue?

7. Lachrymatory-factor synthase is released into the air when you perform a particular daily task. The synthase enzyme converts the amino acid sulfoxides of the item you are working on into sulfenic acid. The unstable sulfenic acid rearranges itself into syn-propanethial-S-oxide. This gets into the air and irritates the lachrymal glands, which then respond by releasing their contents. What would you be doing for this to happen?

8. The Mohs scale of mineral hardness characterizes the scratch resistance of various minerals through the ability of a harder material to scratch a softer material. The large amount of mineral (close to 96 per cent) in 'X' accounts not only for its strength but also for its brittleness. 'X' ranks 5 on the Mohs scale and is made up of hydroxyapatite, which is a crystalline form of calcium phosphate. What is this substance that is found in only one place in the human body?

9. Severe Combined Immunodeficiency (SCID) is a genetic disorder in which the adaptive immune system is defective. The victims are extremely vulnerable to infections, hence they have to be in a controlled environment. In 1976, a film was made with John Travolta playing a person who suffers from SCID. The title of the film alludes to how he has to live his life under constant control. What was the name of the film?

10. According to researchers working on 'Amyotrophic Lateral Sclerosis' (ALS), a neurological disorder, the millions of dollars donated through this unlikely 'challenge' has given them the financial freedom to pursue 'high-risk, high-reward' experiments. Their risk paid off when this freedom allowed them to perform an experiment where they introduced a protein designed to mimic TDP-43 into the neurons of ALS patients, which resulted in the cells coming back to life and becoming fully restored. This could have the potential to slow down or even stop the ill effects of ALS, something that is currently not possible. What challenge was taken by thousands of people and shared on social media in 2014 that brought about the awareness and funds for this research?

11. Zbtb7 is a gene that acts as a master switch for cancer, and is responsible for the proliferation of cancer throughout surrounding cells. The gene, which was first written about in the January 2005 issue of *Nature*,

is unique in that it is needed for other oncogenes to cause cancer. It was originally called 'X', which referred to its full description, 'POK erythroid myeloid ontogenic factor', but it was changed after a lawsuit was threatened by an entertainment company. What is X, of which an augmented reality game version became a rage in 2018?

12. *Gattaca* is a 1997 American science-fiction film starring Ethan Hawke, Uma Thurman and Jude Law. The film presents a dystopian future of discriminatory eugenics, where children are genetically modified to ensure they possess the best hereditary traits of their parents. What does the title *Gattaca* refer to?

13. In cell and molecular biology, the GFP gene is frequently used as a reporter of expression in organisms. Since its discovery by Roger Y. Tsien, Osamu Shimomura, and Martin Chalfie, it has been expressed in many species, such as bacteria, yeasts, fungi, fish and mammals, and even in human cells. The discovery led to the 2008 Nobel Prize in Chemistry. What does GFP stand for, and from which animal, in which it can be clearly visualized, was it first isolated?

14. In 1970, Christiane Nüsslein-Volhard and Eric Wieschaus isolated mutations in genes that control development of the segmented anterior-posterior body axis of the fly, for which they got a Nobel in 1995. These genes code for intercellular signalling molecules, which are denoted by 'Hh'. Hh gets its name

from a (very cute) animal which the fruit fly embryo resembles when it lacks that gene. Fittingly, the gene is found in three types—Desert, Indian and Sonic. What does Hh stand for?

15. In zebrafish, this genetic mutation results in very small ears; in fruit flies the same mutation causes the wings to develop in a swirly pattern. The name of the mutation is a reference to a famous painter who had a troubled life. In case of the zebrafish gene, it subtly references an important event in the person's life, while the fruit fly gene creates a wing pattern reminiscent of one of his most famous works. What is the name of the mutation?

16. A 'borborygmus' is produced by movement of the contents of the gastro-intestinal tract as they are propelled through the small intestine by a series of muscle contractions. They can usually be heard through a stethoscope, but sometimes can be loud enough to be heard outside. It is usually referred to as a sign of a particular condition, but in fact it points to proper functioning of the digestive system. How do we know the borborygmus more commonly, and what is the condition usually affixed to it?

17. Only 10 per cent of all humans have this recessive trait but the number is significantly higher in certain groups, for example 23 per cent of Wimbledon winners in the Open Era, 30 per cent of Test Cricket batsmen and a remarkable 47 per cent among the last fifteen US

presidents. What sinister trait is this that was looked down upon in the Dark Ages?

18. Genetic Use Restriction Technology (GURT) is a method by which plants are genetically modified to cause second-generation seeds to be infertile. This is done to restrict the use of these plants outside the proposed plans. It was also seen as a way for Biotech companies to ensure that farmers kept coming back to them for seeds instead of propagating the crop themselves. What is the name given to these seeds which apparently kill themselves?

19. Phenylthiocarbamide (PTC) is a phenyl ring containing organosulfur thiourea, which has the very interesting property of having a different taste depending on the taster's genes. It can be either practically tasteless or taste very bitter, depending on the dominant genetic trait of the taster. Vegetables from the Brassica genus contain a compound that is almost identical to PTC, and this might explain why certain people have a clear disdain for this vegetable which other people like. What vegetable is this, which US President George Bush Sr once banned in the White House?

20. This substance, scientifically known as 'Cerumen', has antimicrobial properties that reduce the viability of bacteria and fungus in the area where it is found. Unfortunately, people have the habit of removing it on a regular basis, which reduces protection for that organ. One of the ways we use to remove it actually has

been shown to have the negative effect of pushing the cerumen deeper inside, hence worsening the situation. What is this substance that should be removed only under doctor's orders?

ANSWERS

1. Meme
2. The spleen
3. Traumatic acid
4. Draculin
5. Viruses
6. The Mad Hatter from *Alice in Wonderland*
7. Cutting onions
8. Tooth enamel
9. *The Boy in the Plastic Bubble*
10. Ice-bucket Challenge
11. Pokemon
12. The four DNA bases—G, A, T and C
13. Green Fluorescent Protein, Jellyfish
14. Hedgehog
15. Van Gogh mutation
16. Stomach grumble, hunger
17. Left-handedness
18. Suicide seeds
18. Broccoli
20. Ear-wax

2. INSPIRED INVENTIONS I

1. In 1974, a Hungarian professor, Erno X, came up with a certain object to help his students understand three-dimensional problems. Erno had no idea that forty years on, this object would not only be popular around the world with children and adults, but would also be the subject of many international competitions and contests! What colourful invention did Erno spring upon the world, which is known to us all by his last name?

2. René Laënnec was a French doctor who invented an instrument that is now almost synonymous with doctors. Until his idea, doctors needed to touch their patients in order to carry out certain investigations. Laënnec came up with this invention in 1816 in order to minimize physical contact with a patient, apparently a young woman. What was this game-changer for medical examinations?

3. X was a famous American polymath who, among other things, patented the geodesic dome, a dome made up

of triangular structures that were much stronger than conventional rectangular structures. Indeed, this shape became associated so much with him that his name was used to describe specific carbon structures. What is the name of this engineer, architect, cartographer, and activist (to name just a few of the roles he played)?

4. Frederick Banting was a surgeon who was interested in the working of the pancreas. He devised an experiment to prove a theory he had, and hired a physician called Macleod and gave him a lab to work in. After many months, they finally succeeded, and in 1922, they announced their discovery to the world. In 1923, they were granted US patents. Knowing how much this was going to change the world of medicine and how many lives it would benefit, they sold the patents to the University of Toronto for just 1$ each. What is this first ever human protein to be artificially synthesized?

5. Leonardo Da Vinci loved water. He developed plans for floating snowshoes, a breathing device for underwater exploration, and a diving bell that could attack ships from below. All of these came from the same period in time because he had to flee Milan during the Second Italian War in 1499 and settle in another city, where he worked with his mathematician friend Luca Pacioli. He was employed as a military architect and devised methods to defend the city from naval attack. Which city (where he stayed only for one year), unsurprisingly, is the cause for all these aquatic inventions?

6.   Alfred Fielding and Marc Chavannes were two inventors who were attempting to create a three-dimensional plastic wallpaper in 1957. That idea failed, but they found a resourceful use for the item they had invented. It is made with polyethylene film, with a shaped side bonded to a flat side which leads to the formation of the characteristic shape that gives this entity its name. Due to this shape, it provides a cushioning effect to sensitive objects. What is this entity that many people take much pleasure in just destroying one by one?

7.   In around 1908, Thomas Sullivan, a New York merchant specializing in a certain Asian product, started to send samples of the product to his customers in small bags made of silk. His customers thought that these were supposed to be used in the same manner in which they had been using certain metal infusers. Instead of emptying out the contents, they put the entire bag into the pot. When some customers complained that the silk mesh was too fine, Sullivan started making the sachets out of gauze. This was how this product was accidentally discovered. What product is this, that you should find in any store in India?

8.   Wilson Greatbatch was building an oscillator to record heart sounds when he pulled the wrong resistor out of a box. Instead of picking a 10,000-ohm resistor, he accidentally took the 1-megaohm variety. The resulting circuit produced a signal that sounded for 1.8 milliseconds, and then paused for a second and then

gave off a rhythmic electrical pulse. This lead to him patenting a device that generates electrical impulses delivered by electrodes to contract the muscles of a certain vital organ and regulate its electrical conduction system. What life-saving device did Greatbatch invent?

9. Joseph Bramah was an English inventor and locksmith who started out as a cabinetmaker. He went on to devise a pick proof lock which he exhibited in his shop window, offering a reward of 200 guineas to any person who could pick the lock. He also invented an improved toilet (a forebearer of the modern one), a wood-planing machine, a machine for numbering bank notes and the first beer tap. His most notable invention, though, was a device which consists of a cylinder fitted with a sliding piston that exerts a force on a confined liquid, which in turn produces a compressive force on a baseplate. What is this device that is responsible for making our lives easier in many ways?

10. Thomas Jefferson was one of the founding fathers of the United States of America and also a designer who is responsible for designing the Capitol building in Washington D.C. He was also a very inspired inventor, and among his many inventions are a revolving book-stand and a 'Great Clock' powered by the gravitational pull on cannonballs. He is also credited as the inventor of a certain furniture item that he himself used while writing the Declaration of Independence. This item

allows one to rotate 360 degrees while remaining seated in one spot. What did Jefferson invent, that is now an integral part of all offices?

ANSWERS

1. The Rubik's Cube. The professor was Ernō Rubik.
2. Stethoscope
3. Buckminster Fuller
4. Insulin
5. Venice
6. Bubble wrap
7. Teabags
8. Artificial pacemaker for the heart
9. Hydraulic press
10. The swivel chair

3. INSPIRED INVENTIONS II

1. The river Nile was the biggest source of employment for the Egyptians. It had a very regular flooding cycle, which was extremely important to know to ensure that crops did not get wasted. By 2510 BC the Egyptians had invented something to correspond to the annual flooding of the Nile and also help them identify three seasons (inundation, growth and harvest) which were dependent on this. This invention and the version we use now only differ slightly in a few instances, because of Roman interference which happened centuries later. What was this invention that they had inscribed on huge slabs and we now carry around in phones?

2. Egypt shares space with the Sahara Desert and the Libyan Desert and is known for its sweltering summers. The region was also known for insects and other pests. To counter both these issues the Egyptians did something in the summer. But the result of this process was not regarded as aesthetically pleasing, hence they invented a covering entity made with plant

fibre, sheep wool and the original material that was removed in the first place. Some of these coverings had resin and beeswax added, which melted in the sun and added fragrance. What did the Egyptians do and what was the invention to hide this?

3. Numerous ancient Roman structures like the Colosseum, the Forum and the Pantheon are standing today thanks to this Roman invention. It used '*Pozzolana*' or volcanic ash, which is an aluminous and siliceous mixture that reacts with calcium hydroxide at room temperature in the presence of water. After the Roman Empire collapsed, use of this became rare until the technology was redeveloped in the mid-eighteenth century. Today, it is the most widely used man-made material. What civilization-building material is this?

4. This invention by a German goldsmith in the 1400s is a prominent part of the foundation on which modern civilization was built. It served a great role in the industrial revolution, and by then, even the lower classes were able to have access to information and get to know about what was happening around them. The impact of this invention in history was best described by Mark Twain: 'What the world is today, good and bad, it owes to ____.' Who was the inventor and what was this historic invention?

5. Thomas Newcomen was a preacher and an ironmonger in England in the mid-1600s. One of the biggest issues where he lived (Devon) was the flooding of coal and tin

mines. He was engaged in trying to devise and improve ways of pumping out water from flooded mines. In 1712, he finally achieved his dream by building a device that performs mechanical work by using up water in its gaseous phase. This invention is said to have kick-started the industrial revolution, as it went on to power industries and locomotives. What was this invention, which was improved later by James Watt?

6. Hero of Alexandria was a mathematical engineer in the first century who, among other things, invented a wind wheel, early syringes and a standalone fountain. He was also the first to come up with a certain device which we are used to now. He designed a machine where you drop a coin into the slot on top for it to dispense a certain quantity of holy water. This is the very first version of a device that you have most probably used in an airport or a train station. What is it?

7. When this English doctor set up his practice in a small town surrounded by dairy farms, he noticed that a deadly disease plaguing the rest of the country was noticeably absent in his area, especially amongst the population of milkmaids. To prove a theory he had, he called his gardener's eight-year-old son, James, and infected him with a virus taken from one of the infected cows. James went on to recover from this, and also from the actual disease, which too the doctor infected him with. This led to the doctor discovering a process that led to the eradication of that deadly

disease. Who was this doctor and what process did he discover?

8. Alessandro Volta was a professor of physics, who in 1776 discovered and isolated Methane gas for the first time. His contribution was even greater in the invention of his 'voltaic column'. This consisted of alternating disks of zinc and silver separated by cloth soaked in sodium hydroxide. It provided the first source of continuous electric current. Thanks to this column, what is Volta considered the inventor of?

9. Jacob Perkins was initially apprenticed to a goldsmith but soon became a prolific inventor who had forty patents in his name. He invented machines to make nails, bore out cannons and measure the depth of the sea. His greatest invention, though, is thanks to a patent he has for a process which was based off an idea by Oliver Evans. The process, known as Vapor-Compression _____ (VCRs), is a system which uses a circulating liquid which absorbs and removes heat from a space. This process enabled the rise and expansion of large cities in so-called inhospitable areas. Developed countries are heavily dependent on this process to ensure that the population gets its daily quota of food. What process did Perkins invent that changed the world of food?

10. The US military had a tough time keeping ammunition cases dry during World War II. To solve the issue, researchers at Johnson & Johnson came up with a

strong, waterproof three-ply tape which had a fabric mesh between two layers consisting of polyethylene on top and a rubber-based adhesive on the bottom. It proved to be extremely strong, but when required, could be ripped into strips. Its ability to repel water reminded users of a certain waterfowl's waxy feathers, which are immortalized in a popular phrase. This inspired them to give it the name it is popularly known by now. What is this invention that has been shown to have multiple uses in popular culture?

ANSWERS

1. A civil calendar consisting of 365 days and twelve months with thirty days each
2. Shaved their heads, wigs
3. Concrete
4. Gutenberg Press
5. Steam engine
6. Vending machine
7. Edward Jenner, vaccination against smallpox
8. The battery
9. Refrigeration
10. Duct Tape, originally known as 'Duck Tape'

4. DAZZLING DISCOVERIES

1. In 2018, a telescope, located on Mauna Kea in Hawaii, dissected infrared light from Uranus and discovered that cloud-tops on the planet were made up of an incredibly smelly gas. If you landed on Uranus and survived exposure to the -200 degree celsius atmosphere, what gas are you likely to smell?

2. In July 2018, scientists studying how epithelial cells were arranged in some organs discovered that they took on a certain shape in order to accommodate the curvature of the organs. The fascinating part was that this was a shape that was previously undefined in mathematics! The scientists decided to name this shape after the 'scutellum', a triangle-shaped part of a beetle's thorax. What is the name of this brand new shape?

3. John Walker was an English pharmacist who worked with natural ingredients as well as several chemical substances, things that were not used much in medicine back then. In 1827, he was stirring a pot of chemicals that included antimony sulfide and

potassium chlorate. He noticed this dried lump at the end of his mixing stick. To clean it, he tried to rub it against his hearth, but it burst into flames. What idea for an invention did this ignite in Walker's head?

4. This Scottish gentleman can attribute his Nobel Prize to a happy accident. He was experimenting with the influenza virus in his lab and took a two-week vacation. He returned to find a mold on an accidentally contaminated culture plate. In his words: 'When I woke up just after dawn on September 28, 1928, I certainly didn't plan to revolutionize all medicine by discovering the world's first bacteria killer. But I suppose that was exactly what I did.' Who was this (thankfully) careless researcher and what had he discovered?

5. Roy J. Plunkett was a chemist who hoped to create a new variety of chlorofluorocarbons. Once, after an experiment, he and his assistant found what was supposed to be a canister full of gas almost empty except for a few white flakes. Intrigued, Plunkett began at once to experiment with their properties. The new substance proved to be a fantastic lubricant with an extremely high melting point. What had he discovered that makes a daily task much easier?

6. George de Mestral, a life-long inventor, went for a walk in the forest with his dog. An Irish Pointer, its shaggy hair was covered with the prickly heads of a Burdock plant. Being a curious person, he decided to see how this looks under a microscope. What he saw led to

a multi-million-dollar industry, with his invention becoming a worldwide success. What did de Mestral invent that has even made it to spacesuits?

7. Pharmacist John Pemberton just wanted to cure headaches. His two main ingredients were the leaves and nuts of a plant from the Erythroxylaceae family (the species from which cocaine is made). When his lab assistant accidentally mixed the two with carbonated water, he ended up making something which went on to become a multi-billion-dollar empire. What had Pemberton's assistant created, that is now one of the two leading brands in that market worldwide?

8. In 1896, French scientist Henri Becquerel heard about Röntgen's serendipitous discovery of X-rays and started working on an experiment involving a uranium-enriched crystal. He believed that with the help of sunlight, the crystal would burn its image on a photographic plate. With dark clouds rolling in, Becquerel packed up his gear and decided to continue his research on another, sunny day. Later, he retrieved the crystal from a darkened drawer, but the image burned on the plate was 'fogged.' After further analysis with the help of a science super-couple, he was awarded a Nobel Prize for enlightening us on which natural phenomenon?

9. In the late 1980s, scientists at a laboratory hypothesized that by selectively blocking an enzyme called phosphodiesterase type 5, they could relax the blood

vessels of the heart and treat Angina Pectoris (spasms in the heart's coronary arteries). The company developed a pill named UK92480 to help constrict these arteries and relieve pain. The pill failed in its primary purpose, but the secondary side effect was startling. Initially patented and sold as 'Revatio', a cardiovascular drug, it hardly made a presence in the market. The same drug was renamed and sold as the first oral drug for a completely different problem. This time, the sales hit a billion dollars easily. What was this new drug they had accidentally discovered?

10. This gentleman was born in what is now Uttarkhand, in 1857. He wanted to become a writer, but his father enrolled him in a medical college in London. He spent most of his time there writing poems and plays. After graduating he became a surgeon on a ship. In 1883 he was posted in Bengaluru, where he noticed that by limiting access to water he could control mosquito populations. On 20 August 1897, he discovered something in a mosquito. This led to him becoming the first Nobel Laureate born outside of Europe. Who was this doctor and which disease's vector had he discovered?

11. The Mpemba effect is a temperature-dependent process in which hot water can freeze faster than cold water. It is named after Erasto Bartholomeo Mpemba, who discovered this effect when he was thirteen years old and in school. He noticed it when he was in cooking

class and was trying to make something faster than his classmates. What popular item was Mpemba trying to make in the freezer when he discovered this unusual physical phenomena?

12. Friedrich Miescher was a Swiss physician who initially wanted to be a priest. Since he had a hearing problem, he chose to follow a career in medical research, which would not need him to interact with patients. He joined a lab where he was given the task of researching the composition of white blood cells. He experimented and isolated a new molecule, 'nuclein', which he determined to be made up of hydrogen, oxygen, nitrogen and phosphorus—and there was a unique ratio of phosphorus to nitrogen. What had Miescher 'discovered', which would finally be understood close to two hundred years later?

13. Henry Bigelow was a famous doctor in Boston who specialized in treatment of kidney stones. In 1846, he published an article titled 'Insensibility during Surgical Operations Produced by Inhalation'. This was later selected as the most important article in the *New England Journal of Medicine*. He had discovered the effects of a certain organic compound on patients, which made it easier to do the operations. What 'field' had Bigelow discovered and what was the compound?

14. This Russian chemist investigated the composition of petroleum, and helped to found the first oil refinery in Russia. His greatest contribution, though, was a

discovery he made when he was arranging chemical elements by atomic weight. He realized that elements with similar properties could be grouped together. Using this, he could predict the properties of some already discovered elements, and also of those yet to be discovered. Who was this far-thinking chemist and what was his discovery?

15. William Herschel was a German musician and astronomer. He constructed his own telescope when he was thirty-six years old, in 1774, and he went on to catalogue more than 5,000 heavenly objects. In 1781, he discovered the planet Uranus, which was the first planet to be discovered in the modern era. His greatest discovery, though, happened when he was studying the heating effect of different colours of light by using a prism to produce a spectrum of colours, and thermometers to measure their heating effect. What did he discover that is now used in many areas, including tracking, heating, meteorology, astronomy etc.?

16. Isidor Isaac Rabi won the 1944 Nobel Prize in Physics for his discovery of a phenomenon where nuclei in a strong constant magnetic field are perturbed by a weak oscillating magnetic field and respond by producing an electromagnetic signal with a frequency characteristic of the magnetic field at the nucleus. This led to the development of many processes that accelerated the rate of discovery in physics, especially

after the invention of Spectroscopy, which was based on this phenomenon. What did Rabi discover (which abbreviates to NMR)?

17. Austrian botanist Friedrich Reinitzer was examining the physico chemical properties of various derivatives of cholesteryl benzoate in 1888 when he discovered a certain entity. This is actually a state of matter that has properties between those of conventional liquids and those of solid crystals. Thanks to his discovery, we have the now ubiquitous electronic displays. What had this botanist discovered?

18. A group of South African lime quarry workers discovered a skull in 1924. They thought it was of an ape and handed it over to Raymond Dart. He saw that the spinal column was connected below the skull and not at the back and realized that it was a human, and then found that it was 3.7 million years old. Named Australopithecus, the specimen's brain size was roughly 35 per cent of that of a modern human. Why was this discovery of Australopithecus an important event in anthropology?

19. Swedish pharmacist Carl Wilhelm Scheele had identified molybdenum, tungsten, barium, hydrogen, chlorine, the organic acids tartaric, oxalic, uric, lactic, and citric, as well as hydrofluoric, hydrocyanic, and arsenic acids. But in every case it was someone else who was given the credit, as he had not published his findings. His biggest discovery was in 1772, when he

was analyzing the properties of manganese (IV) oxide and discovered something that he named 'Fire Air'. He wrote a manuscript called *Treatise on Air and Fire* which, unfortunately, his publisher did not publish till 1777. In 1774, the same gas was identified by Joseph Priestley, who was able to publish his paper in the same year. What did they both discover, which is a gas we owe our lives to?

20. Jan Evangelista Purkyně was a Czech anatomist who coined the terms 'protoplasm' for the fluid substance of a cell and 'plasma' for the liquid component of the blood, and discovered the Purkinje effect in human eyes, Purkinje cells (large neurons), Purkinje fibres (a type of fibrous tissue) and the Purkinje shift (the change in the brightness of red and blue colours as light intensity decreases gradually at dusk). But the discovery he made with the most practical applications was encapsulated in a thesis he wrote in 1823, where he laid out nine principal configuration groups of a certain human feature. Till today, it is one of the most vital components in crime solving. What did Purkyně write his thesis on?

21. In 1978, Dr Amar _____ was taking a flight and was looking forward to plugging in headphones into the armrest of his seat, a relatively recent development. He was sorely disappointed, however, when the noise of the jet almost drowned out what he was listening to. Craving better sound, and having quite some

experience in this line, he and his company went on to design the revolutionary item that is now their flagship product. What is this product, and what is Dr Amar's last name, which is associated with an entire range of products?

22. A four-month-old, Theo, was involved in an accident that resulted in a head injury and subsequent hydrocephalus (fluid accumulation in the brain). A shunt was put in place to drain the fluid, but the boy's parents were horrified to discover that the shunt would get blocked. The father, a writer for adults at that point, got in touch with a friend of his who made miniature aircrafts, and a surgeon. The trio developed a much superior shunt that prevented backflows and was also significantly cheaper. They continued to work on producing this even when Theo stabilized (he grew up to be a healthy adult). The shunt came to be known as the Wade-_____-Till shunt. Having given this miraculous gift to innumerable families around the world, Theo's writer father went on to produce works that gave and continue to give great joy to children today. Who was this brilliant writer and inventor?

23. This inventor held over 355 patents when he died in 1896. As a chemist he had helped create various products such as artificial silk, artificial leather, synthetic rubber etc. However, he was best known for his breakthrough in controlling the previously highly unpredictable explosive liquid, nitroglycerin. Despite

this being his most successful patent, the inventor has become immortal for creating something else that he hoped people would remember him by instead! Who was this prolific inventor, whose name is a goal in many fields of human endeavour?

24. In the series *Star Trek*, Captain Kirk is shown using a communication device for voice communication. Engineer Martin Cooper cited this as the inspiration for a device he created when working with a certain company. What absolutely game-changing device was this and what company first manufactured it?

25. According to legend, Galileo Galilei wanted to demonstrate that two items of different masses, if dropped together, would fall at the same time. So he took two cannonballs of different sizes and dropped them from the top floor of this iconic building. The reasons for him choosing this particular building was a) it was in his city b) the unique nature of this building allowed him to drop the balls by hand without their fall being obstructed by any part of the building. Many scholars think this was just a thought experiment and did not actually happen, as air resistance would play a major role in any such experiment. Finally, in 1971, Commander David Scott proved this right by dropping a 1.32 kg hammer and a 0.03 kg falcon feather from a height of 1.6 metres in a place where there is absolutely no air resistance. As the video clearly shows, both of them fall at the same time, hence proving Galileo

right more than three hundred years later and about 384,400 km away. Where did Galileo want to do the experiment and where was it done finally?

ANSWERS

1. Hydrogen sulphide
2. Scutoid
3. Matchsticks
4. Alexander Fleming, Penicillin
5. Teflon used in nonstick cookware
6. Velcro
7. Coca-Cola
8. Radioactivity
9. Viagra
10. Ronald Ross discovered malaria parasites in the anopheles mosquito
11. Ice cream
12. DNA
13. Anaesthetics, Ether
14. Dmitri Mendeleev, The Periodic Table
15. Infra red rays
16. Nuclear Magnetic Resonance
17. Liquid crystals
18. The earliest human ancestor was discovered
19. Oxygen
20. Fingerprints
21. Noise-cancelling headphones; Bose

22. Roald Dahl
23. Alfred Nobel
24. The cell phone, Motorola
25. Leaning Tower of Pisa, The moon

5. CURIOUS CHEMISTRY

1. This mineral is an excellent conductor of electricity and also has the unique ability to absorb neutrons. Consequently, it is used to control the speed of nuclear fission in reactors. It has such a high melting point that it is used as a crucible for melting metals. When combined with other materials, it is extremely strong and is found everywhere from F1 cars to plane fuselages. You would most probably encounter this mineral in a very soft form as part of an object you would have used daily in school, but under a misnomer. What mineral is this?

2. The word 'silver' comes from the Anglo-Saxon word 'seolfor'. It is a popular myth that there is no word that rhymes with silver but 'chilver', which means a female lamb, has been in dictionaries for quite a while. It is a popular element used to make cutlery, as it actually has germicidal properties and has the ability to kill bacteria. Silver is exceptionally shiny, and it is the most reflective element, which makes it

useful in mirrors, telescopes, microscopes and solar cells. Polished silver reflects 95 per cent of the visible light spectrum. Silver's chemical name and symbol though, are based on another name, whose roots are in the Sanskrit word '*argunas*' which means 'shining'. What are the chemical symbol and name for silver?

3. This is an essential element needed for life which was accidentally discovered by a French chemist while he was making saltpetre for use in the Napoleonic Wars. It sublimates (changes from a solid to a gaseous state directly) easily and gives off a purple vapour—in fact, its name is borrowed from the Greek word for purple. Found everywhere from disinfectants to CT scans, this is the least reactive halogen element. Although it is technically a non-metal, it exhibits some metallic qualities. The human body requires this element in minute quantities to manufacture certain vital hormones. What is this element's name?

4. Tungsten is a rare metal that is noted for its robustness—it has the highest melting point of all discovered elements at 3422°C. This makes it excellent for use in light bulbs, X-ray tubes and welding electrodes. Its other name is derived from '*lupispuma*', which translates into English as '____'s froth', and is a reference to the large amounts of tin consumed by the mineral during its extraction (like the ____ eats sheep). What is the one-letter chemical symbol for tungsten

which is based on this second name?

5. This is a colourless, odourless, tasteless noble gas. From 1960 to 1983, the official length of a meter was defined by the 605 nm wavelength of the orange spectral line of this element. It was discovered in 1898 by Sir William Ramsay, a Scottish chemist, and Morris Travers, an English chemist, in residue left from evaporating nearly all components of liquid air. It is considered to be a non-toxic asphyxiant and has a narcotic potency seven times greater than air. You may have seen its effects in popular culture on a particular alien character, who is seemingly invincible except when they come into contact with this element. What element is this that entered popular culture in the 1940s?

6. The ancient Romans believed that Cupid's arrows were tipped with this material (perhaps the earliest association between this object and romantic love). Its history is quite remarkable, as the demand and exorbitant pricing for it are, thanks entirely to clever marketing and successful advertising campaigns. This object is artificially manufactured in tons and used for industrial cutting, drilling and polishing. What is this object with a chequered history that is ubiquitous in film and literature?

7. This is the heaviest known alkaline earth metal and is the only radioactive member in its group. This element was once used in watches, nuclear panels, aircraft switches, clocks, and instrument dials. In the

mid-1920s, a lawsuit was filed by five dying painters. The dial painters routinely licked their brushes to give them a fine point, thereby ingesting this element. This exposure caused serious health effects and eventually led to bone cancer. This is because the body treats this element as calcium and deposits it in the bones, where radioactivity degrades marrow and mutates the bone cells. Which element is this, which has such disastrous consequences?

8. This metal is the only registered antibacterial metal (bacteria die upon coming into contact with this metal) and is also one of the only two non-silvery metals in the world. One of these is gold. What is this other, antibacterial one that is also an excellent conductor of heat and electricity?

9. This molecule happens to be flame-retardant flame when heated, the phosphate-rich structure removes water and forms a flame-resistant carbon residue. Further, the nitrogen bases release ammonia, which forms a protective shield that resists the flames. Scientists are now experimenting on coating substances with this molecule to make them flame retardant. If this results in flame-retardant clothing, then people will have this molecule on the inside and outside! What is this hardy molecule that seems essential for survival?

10. This person studied Chemistry at Oxford and went on to work as a research chemist for four years, while also studying to become a barrister. When elected as

their country's prime minister, they made history for a certain reason. However, in addition to this, it's also worth bearing in mind that they were the first (and as of 2019, the only) PM of their country to have an undergraduate degree in science! Who is this person, who specialized in X-ray crystallography?

11. Bee stings can be soothed by applying Milk of Magnesia or bicarbonate of soda. This involves a very basic concept in Chemistry. What reaction does this involve and what does this tell us about bee stings?

12. A well-known saying goes, 'one rotten apple spoils the barrel.' This is quite true—and interestingly it is true for a variety of fruits, including pears and apricots. This is because the rotten (or even ripe) fruit releases something that speeds up the process in surrounding fruit. What is this chemical that is released?

13. Linus Pauling is known to be the only person in the world, as of 2019, to have won two Nobel Prizes all for himself! (That is, he didn't have to share them with anyone.) He won the Nobel Prize in Chemistry for discoveries that had implications in multiple fields, including playing a key role in the discovery of DNA. His second Nobel, which was not awarded for science, was related to a very important activity. What was this Nobel Prize and why was it awarded to Pauling?

14. According to researchers, this substance causes stored fat to migrate into the bloodstream and leaves higher reserves of glycogen in the liver and muscles. This

means that athletes would be able to burn fat for the bulk of their performance and be able to use the glycogen only when they most need it, extending their performance. Due to its properties, this substance was banned from the Olympics between 1984 and 2004. However, this ban was subsequently removed. One of the reasons for this was that the substance is commonly found in many food and drink items, and was likely to lead to false charges of doping. What is this substance that large numbers of people around the world are likely to ingest for more productivity, whether or not they are athletes?

15. In addition to the above, the Olympics bans many other substances that might give performers an unfair advantage or enhance performance and maintains a strict list of banned substances. What is the name given to any of these performance-boosting drugs?

16. This marvellous substance is known to survive unspoilt for millennia. Archaeologists have discovered containers of this substance in pyramids and found them to be perfectly edible! The weirdly long life of this product can be explained by a variety of factors working together. Its high sugar content essentially makes it have very little moisture naturally, which discourages a lot of bacteria. Secondly, it is highly acidic, thereby making it even more unfriendly to bacteria. Finally, in the process through which it is created, hydrogen peroxide, an antiseptic product,

is produced. This is one of the reasons why many civilizations have used this product as a medicine as well. What is this amazing product?

17. This element was named eka-iodine by Mendeleev since it lay below iodine in his periodic table, and he predicted its properties. However, the element itself was not properly discovered until the 1940s, and even today, is hard to study as its isotopes have a very short half-life and it is believed to be the rarest element in the earth's crust! Scientist's estimate that at any point, the entire crust of the earth contains only about 28-30 mg of this substance. What is the name we now know this element by, which comes from the Greek word for 'unstable'?

18. Titin protein is the largest known protein in the human body and also has the largest number of exons in a single gene. It ensures that muscles are elastic (which is essential to any movement). But all this apart, Titin also holds an interesting record in the world of chemistry and language. What is special about the chemical name for this protein?

19. Jean-Frédéric Joliot and _____ _____ were husband and wife who won the 1935 Nobel Prize in Chemistry for their work on artificially producing radioactive isotopes. That is, they took substances that were not radioactive and produced radioactive isotopes of these substances by bombarding them with alpha particles. Who was Jean-Frédéric's wife and why was it natural

that this was their field of work?

20. In 1856, an eighteen-year-old student, William Perkin, was given a task by his professor to synthesize quinine. He failed at doing so but when cleaning up the flask with alcohol later, he discovered a purplish-bluish substance which he called aniline. He later patented it and sold it under a different name, 'Mauveine'. What was this the very first version of and what colour did it give rise to?

ANSWERS

1. Graphite
2. Argentum (Ag)
3. Iodine
4. W (Wolfram)
5. Krypton
6. Diamonds
7. Radium
8. Copper
9. DNA
10. Margaret Thatcher
11. Acid-base neutralization reaction; bee stings are acidic
12. Ethylene gas
13. The Nobel Peace Prize, for his pacifist efforts during the Cold War
14. Caffeine
15. Ergogenic aids

16. Honey
17. Astatine (from the Greek 'Astatos')
18. Widely considered the longest word in the English language with 189,819 letters!
19. Irène Curie, the daughter of Marie and Pierre Curie
20. The very first synthetic dye, Mauve

6. MURDEROUS MEDICINE

1. Many cultures and civilizations have known for thousands of years about the properties of salicylates—for example, the medicinal property of white willow, which contains derivatives of this substance. However, it was only in the 1800s that this chemical was first isolated in a lab, and only in the late 1800s that the form in which we know it today was patented. What is the generic name by which we know this painkiller?

2. In 1828, in Edinburgh (Scotland), bodies would often be robbed from graves, and relatives started standing guard over the graves of family members. This, of course, made it hard to steal them. So, in 1828, began a series of baffling murders carried out by William Burke and William Hare. They were finally discovered, arrested and sentenced for these murders. But what was the reason Burke and Hare (along with others) robbed graves or (by themselves) murdered people?

3. This is an old therapeutic practice that is still used in

the world of modern medicine. While it was initially used in the belief that various fluids in the body had to be balanced and this therapy could be used to draw away excess fluid, it is used today as a means of 'microsurgery' to reduce swollen veins around the site of surgery. The process also injects some anesthesia and some mild anticoagulants into the blood, which is beneficial to the doctor. Known as 'hirudotherapy', what is this seemingly awful practice?

4. While many urban legends claim that this substance can be used as a substitute for IV-fluid, medical research has shown that it should only be a last resort. This is because the composition of the substance is high potassium–low sodium, the opposite of the fluid in our blood. It also contains calcium and magnesium, which could cause complications in patients with weak kidneys. One of the reasons people believe this can be used is that until its container is cracked open, it is fully enclosed and, therefore, sterile. What is this liquid that *may* be an emergency intravenous-fluid but is definitely not generally recommended?

5. In ancient India, a specific procedure was used to close incisions in abdominal surgeries (of the intestine). A certain entity would be used to hold the two ends of a wound together and then cut off, so that the part that was holding the wound closed would remain. Once the external incision was stitched up using thread, the stomach's juices would ensure that the entities holding

the wound together slowly dissolved over time, by which time the wound would have healed shut. What were these early forms of 'staples'?

6. What work from ancient times contains detailed descriptions of surgery based on the type of surgery (eight kinds—excision, scarification, puncturing, exploration, extraction, evacuation and suturing) and also contains detailed descriptions of over 120 surgical instruments as well as the order in which they must be laid for a surgery? The title of this work contains the name of one of history's most famous surgeons.

7. Red blood cells do not have an important cell component that most other cells do. This leaves extra space in the cell to carry around oxygen through the body (an important function!). What is this specific component that is missing in the RBCs?

8. Born Loretta Pleasant in 1920, this lady went to Johns Hopkins Hospital, which was the only hospital in the area that treated black patients at that time. The physician discovered a fast-growing cancerous tumor on her cervix. Samples of her cells were obtained without her knowledge or permission and sent for scientific research. These cells had an extraordinary ability to grow and stay alive in any condition. It is estimated that Loretta's immortal cells currently live in labs in every continent and have been used to test drugs that treat thousands of diseases. Only in the 2010 was her contribution to science finally recognized and

today the name she took on, Henrietta Lacks, lives on in the immortal cell line. What is the name of this cell line, which we are indebted to Lacks for?

9. In order to prove that the bacteria *Heliobacter pylori* could cause a particularly painful condition, an Australian doctor named Barry J. Marshall grew a petri dish containing cultured *Helicobacter pylori* taken from the stomach of a patient. He then drank the culture, developed the condition, and successfully treated it with antibiotics. He won a Nobel Prize for the outcome of this brave experiment in 2005. What is this condition, which was thought to have been brought on by stress earlier?

10. Cannabis vapours (with later additions of aconitum), opium, varying mixtures of wine and herbs and carotid compression were all used for a specific purpose that we immediately associate with surgery today. What end-result did these various substances or physical acts produce that might have made a surgeon's (and a patient's!) life easier?

11. In the 1800s, cholera was one of the most dreaded diseases. It would cause diarrhoea and severe dehydration. Very few people survived it, and antibiotics had not yet been invented to battle this disease. During an epidemic in 1832, Dr Thomas Latta, who was battling to save an old woman from dehydration, had a desperate plan in mind, based on an idea suggested by Dr W.B. O'Shaughnessy.

Although this did not save his patient, it did produce temporary improvement. Dr Latta used this procedure on other patients with better results. The basic idea behind his procedure was to help his patients fight dehydration by directly introducing fluids into blood. Unfortunately, when the epidemic ended and Dr Latta died, the procedure disappeared for close to thirty years. What was this procedure, which is used quite commonly today in hospitals to replace fluid loss and is noted for delivering the fluid 'drop by drop'?

12. This individual was one of the first (and most famous) people to argue that all illnesses had natural causes, rather than blaming supernatural occurrences. He advocated patient-centred medicine and that healers should be clinicians, making close observations and using rational thinking processes. He also emphasized on the moral and ethical dimensions of medical care. Who was this pioneering healer, who plays a key role in the life of doctors even today?

13. Abu Bakhr Al-Razi was a physician in the ninth–tenth century AD who wrote a wide-ranging treatise on medicine called the *Kitab al-hawifi'l-tibb*. This book contained the first detailed description of a deadly disease which terrorized people for centuries before abruptly being wiped out in less than fifty years when the WHO developed a programme to target it. What disease was Al-Razi the first to accurately describe?

14. Conjunctivitis is inflammation of the outermost layer

of the white part of the eye and the inner surface of the eyelid. The most common infectious causes are viral followed by bacterial, and it easily spreads between people. In the early 1950s, the adenovirus responsible for it was supposed to have been discovered at the Government Ophthalmic Hospital in Egmore, Chennai, which is the second oldest ophthalmic hospital in the world. This led to this disease getting a particular name. What is this common name for conjunctivitis?

15. There is a rare genetic disorder called 'Porphyria' which makes people extremely sensitive to sunlight, leaving abrasions on the skin. It turns their urine a purplish-red colour and also increases hair growth while tightening and shrinking the skin, which makes one look younger. When the skin around the mouth tightens it makes the canine teeth more prominent. Eating garlic makes all this worse! Which mythical character do scientists think could have been suffering from this disease?

16. In older individuals, sometimes there is a rupture of the proximal head of the biceps tendon. This is caused by degenerative changes brought on by old age within the tendon that lead to structural failure. If this happens, the patients experience a bulge only in that part of the arm. This reaction is termed after a certain cartoon character that seems to have this issue. After which famous character, who is supposed to gain his strength from a certain vegetable, is this reaction named?

17. This was a genetically transmitted disease which was present prominently in Europe during the nineteenth and twentieth centuries. Queen Victoria's son Prince Leopold and two of his sisters carried this disease, which was passed on over subsequent generations to royal households across Spain, Germany and Russia. This was one reason it was called 'The Royal Disease.' What is the name of this otherwise rare disorder in which the blood lacks sufficient clotting proteins?

18. After a prolonged struggle by a few NGOs and individuals, the Indian government made amendments to the 'Indian Medical Council (Professional Conduct, Etiquette and Ethics) Regulations, 2002, to enforce a certain small but substantial rule to be followed by doctors. As one doctor pointed out, 'The move is in the best interest of the patients, but in an environment where any doctor at any given time is flooded with patients, this system may take a little time to get used to.' What change is this that makes life easier for pharmacists?

19. In the 1950s, an Australian doctor developed appendicitis when on duty at a certain station and went through immense trouble before he could get help. In 1961, when a Russian doctor had the same issue at the same place, he used local anaesthetic and a small mirror and successfully removed his own appendix (since he was the only doctor around for miles). Since this incident, all doctors who are stationed in this place

are required to have their appendix and sometimes even their wisdom teeth removed as a precaution. What place is this that requires such drastic measures?

20. When this disease first surfaced, the English called it the 'French disease', the French called it the 'Spanish disease', the Germans called it the 'French evil', the Russians called it the 'Polish disease', the Poles called it the 'Turkish disease', the Turks called it the 'Christian disease' and Japan called it 'Chinese pox.' The disease is caused by the bacterium *Treponema pallidum* and spread by intimate contact between humans. It has so many different symptoms that are similar to other diseases that it was known as 'the great imitator.' What disease is this that, according to WHO, had affected 45.4 million people in 2015?

21. An American study done on brain and nervous system disorders concluded that athletes of a certain sport were three to four times more likely to contract Alzheimer's disease, Parkinson's disease and Lou Gehrig's disease (ALS) than an average American. These disorders affect nerve function, resulting in loss of movement or memory. One of the main complaints was Chronic Traumatic Encephalopathy (CTE), which occurs in people who've had multiple concussions. Which sport is this that has such a high susceptibility to neurological disorders, even though the players seem to be wearing extensive protective padding?

22. The World Health Organisation (WHO) has warned

that the use of tanning beds, i.e. devices that are used to develop an artificial tan (not from direct exposure to the sun), is dangerous as the lamps used in this process emit UVA and UVB radiation. This is associated with a significant increase in risk for a cancer that affects the largest organ of the human body. What kind of cancer can tanning beds cause?

23. It is believed that the earliest version of this device was invented by German orthopaedist Bernhard Heine, to cut bone. He called it an 'osteotome' and it had links of chains with small cutting teeth moving around a guiding blade. It was further improved by two Scottish doctors as a surgical tool to aid in the process of difficult childbirth. Only much later was it embraced by the timber industry, where it is a vital instrument now. What instrument is this?

24. Doctors in Ancient Rome used an early form of electrotherapy to successfully treat neurological conditions such as epilepsy and migraines. They administered the charges by placing a certain animal on the patient's head. These animals come from the genus Torpedo, the name of which comes from the Latin word '*Torpere*' meaning to stiffen or paralyze—which is what used to happen when anyone accidentally stepped on one of these animals. What animals, which are completely made of cartilage, are these?

25. People used to believe (and perhaps some still do!) that mental health was affected by the phases of the

moon. According to this theory, mental illness worsens during the full moon phases. Of course, various studies of psychiatric illnesses around the full moon have disproved this theory. But it was so prevalent for a while that one of the words we use to describe insanity is derived from the Latin word for moon! What is this term that you've probably used to describe someone as being mad?

26. Alcoholism is such a huge issue in this country that alcohol abuse costs the country half a million deaths a year, most of them men of working age, which leads to billions of dollars of loss in productivity. The male life expectancy is just sixty, thanks to this issue. In this country, many doctors 'treat' alcoholism by surgically implanting a small capsule into their patients. The capsules react so severely with alcohol that once the patient touches a single drop, they instantly acquire an excruciating illness and sometimes it could even be fatal. Which country is this, which has such tragic issues with alcohol—especially vodka?

27. Ernst Moro was an Austrian pediatrician who discovered that breast-fed children have stronger bactericidal activity in their blood than bottle-fed ones. His biggest contribution was his carrot soup. Known as Moro's Carrot soup, he peeled and pureed carrots in water and cooked them for an hour. Then he added salt and served the result. This simple dish exponentially decreased the death of babies from a

then-deadly (now simple) issue. Of what unfortunate digestive issue did Moro's carrot soup save German babies from dying?

28. This disease has been plaguing mankind for thousands of years. Egyptians had recorded its symptoms on papyrus more than 3000 years back. The very first clinical test for this disease was in India, where ants were used for confirming the diagnosis. Even during the later centuries, European doctors used to test the urine of patients to confirm this disease. What problem is this, which is one of the fastest-growing diseases thanks to the increase in the sedentary lifestyle of humans?

29. In 5,000 years of medical history, only two diseases have been completely eradicated. One of them is rinderpest, which was an infectious viral disease in cattle. There was a major antiviral campaign from the mid-1900s, and finally in 2011, the United Nations FAO confirmed that the disease was fully wiped out. The other was an infectious disease caused by one of two virus variants, *Variola major* and *Variola minor*. The earliest record of this disease was in Egyptian mummies from the third century BC, and the last confirmed case was in 1977. In that time period, the disease had killed close to 500 million people. What disease was this that was finally certified as eradicated by WHO in 1980?

30. Melatonin is a hormone released by the pineal gland

that regulates sleep and wakefulness in the body. It is vital for the synchronization of the circadian rhythm and even blood-pressure regulation. It has been proven that light from a recently popular artificial device hampers the production of melatonin and thereby interferes with the sleep cycle. Unfortunately, nowadays people seem to spend more and more time with this device just before they go to sleep, hence worsening the situation. What device is thus responsible for the loss of sleep in people nowadays?

ANSWERS

1. Aspirin
2. To provide cadavers to an unscrupulous doctor (Robert Knox) for medical research
3. Bloodletting through leeches (specific species of leeches are used to suck away excess blood)
4. Coconut water
5. Ants
6. The *Sushruta Samhita*
7. Nucleus
8. HeLa cells
9. Stomach ulcer
10. These were all used as anaesthetics, to numb or knock out a patient
11. The intravenous injection of fluid directly into blood or 'IV drip'

12. Hippocrates, after whom the Hippocratic oath is named
13. Smallpox
14. Madras Eye
15. Vampires or Dracula
16. Popeye
17. Haemophilia
18. Write prescriptions in CAPITAL LETTERS
19. Antarctica
20. Syphilis
21. American football
22. Skin cancer
23. Chainsaw
24. Electric rays
25. Lunacy/lunatic
26. Russia
27. Diarrhoea
28. Diabetes
29. Smallpox
30. Mobile phones

7. PHIZZYING PHYSICS

1. *Dead of Night* is a 1945 British horror film in which a young architect goes to a cottage and meets strangers who he has seen in his dreams before. On telling his story he gets strangled, but just before he dies he wakes up from a dream and the whole thing happens again. Basically the film changes but ends up the same and could continue for eternity. This inspired three scientists in the theatre—Gold, Bondi and Hoyle, who had met while working at a radar station that had been erected to warn about bombing in London. They came up with a revolutionary theory that explained a failed concept proposed by Albert Einstein fifteen years earlier as an alternative to the Big Bang Theory. What is this theory, which is now almost abandoned?

2. The moon is 3,747 km across. The sun is 375 times bigger at 1.39 million km across. The moon is currently 384,400 km from Earth. The sun is 390 times further at 149.6 million km. This extraordinarily close coincidence is responsible for what optical illusion?

3. On 21 April, 1820, during a lecture, Hans Christian Ørsted noticed a compass needle deflected from magnetic north when an electric current from a battery was switched on and off. He began intensive research and soon showed that electric current produces a circular magnetic field as it flows through a wire. This heralded the beginning of a new field that led to scientific innovation which accelerated technology rapidly. What important scientific property is credited to Ørsted?

4. The Large Hadron Collider has had an eventful existence since it was first switched on in 2008. At that time, the LHC had to be shut down due to a helium leak. When it was finally back up and running in 2009, it had to be shut down again when a section started overheating. Investigations revealed a surprising possible source for the power failure that had caused the overheating, although CERN later published a clarification stating that it was all circumstantial evidence and it was likely just an electrical failure. What was this strange object that was supposed to have nearly become toast?

5. In yet another unfortunate incident, the LHC lost power again, when wiring connected to a 66,000 volt transformer was destroyed. This time there was no doubting the cause of the damage. What had brought down one of the most powerful machines in the world?

6. A famous scientist predicted that contrary to popular imagination, 'black holes' were not really black. They

theoretically proved that these entities emitted light across the spectrum! What is the name given to this radiation from Black Holes, named after the scientist?

7. This scientist is credited with two important scientific breakthroughs. One is the discovery of methane, which eventually led to the production of cheaper fuels. The other is an invention that involved copper and zinc discs stacked on top of each other with weak acid in between each pair. Who was this amazing scientist and what was the name of his invention, which revolutionized science?

8. In 1903, three scientists were awarded the Nobel Prize in Physics for work on a certain phenomenon known as 'Becquerel rays'. Two of the scientists had also done seminal work related to this by discovering and isolating two new elements. However, this was not mentioned in their citation, as certain chemists on the Nobel committee had surmised that that work by itself might also earn them a Nobel in Chemistry (it did!). Who were these three scientists?

9. John Bardeen was a physicist who had done his doctoral thesis on the behaviour of electrons in metal. When he joined Bell Labs as a researcher, he was able to provide his colleagues with valuable insights that led to the creation of the world's first semiconductor amplifier (they called this a transistor). This discovery revolutionized science and technology. Bardeen then went on to solve a problem that had stumped physicists

such as Albert Einstein and Richard Feynman—the problem of superconductivity, where at close to 0 degrees, metals freely allow the passage of current. His magnificent scientific achievements earned Bardeen a distinction that is still unique in 2019. What is this distinction?

10. This amazing astronomer provided evidence for the theory that other galaxies are visible to us. Using light variations in stars in the Andromeda nebula, this scientist measured how far away the nebula was and proved that it lay well outside our own galaxy and was, therefore, another galaxy—and not simply a cloud cluster in our own galaxy. He is now considered instrumental in establishing the field of Extragalatic Astronomy and is considered one of the greatest cosmologists. What was this astronomer's name, which anyone with an interest in stargazing is sure to know?

11. Paul Dirac is widely considered one of the greatest British theoretical physicists. He came up with an equation that combined quantum mechanics and Einstein's theory of relativity. He realized later that his equation predicted the existence of particles that had mirror-image antiparticles i.e. nearly identical properties but opposite charge. This discovery predicted the existence of something that is now taken for granted as a part of the universe. What had Paul Dirac predicted, which was proved experimentally by

the time he won a Nobel Prize in Physics with Erwin Schrdödinger?

12. There are two gold-plated copper phonograph records, within an aluminium cover that has an ultra-pure sample of Uranium-238 electroplated on to it. Etched on the surface is the line 'To the makers of music— all worlds, all times.' The records contain sounds such as music by Bach, Beethoven, Blind Willie Johnson, Chuck Berry, Kesarbai Kerkar as well as the sounds of surf, wind, birds, footsteps and laughter. There are also images of the solar system, DNA, human anatomy, food, architecture and portraits. They were all chosen to represent life on Earth as it was in 1977. Right now, they are further away from us than any human-made object ever. Where would one find these two records?

13. This outstanding scientist was largely self-taught. He worked in a bookbindery and would read many of the books that came in for binding. After attending a talk by the famous physicist Sir Humphrey Davy, he approached him for work and was hired based on the meticulous notes he had made from the lecture. While he is best remembered for his pioneering work in the field of electricity and magnetism, he also worked as a chemist and is famous for liquefying various gases and discovering benzene. As his fame grew, the British government asked him for advice on chemical weapons during the Crimean war, which he refused to give on ethical grounds. Who was this magnificent

scientist, who was also a very decent human being?

14. The 'Wall of Death' is a death-defying event in carnival shows and circuses where motorists and car drivers ride/drive and perform stunts along the walls of a barrel-shaped wooden or metal cylinder. This is facilitated by two key basic concepts in physics—one is the resistance that one surface or object encounters when moving over another, and the other is a force that appears to act on a body moving in a circular path, directed away from the centre around which the body is moving. What are these two fundamental concepts that keep these daredevils alive?

15. These heavenly spectacle result from emissions of photons in the Earth's upper atmosphere from ionized nitrogen atoms regaining an electron, and oxygen and nitrogen atoms returning from an excited state to a ground state. They are ionized and the excitation energy is lost by the emission of a photon of light. Named after the Roman goddess of the dawn, when it happens in the southern hemisphere it is suffixed by the name of the only continent completely in that hemisphere. What are these two beautiful natural phenomena known as?

16. The *Annus Mirabilis* papers are four papers of a certain physicist published in the *Annalen der Physik* journal in 1905. These four articles contributed substantially to the foundations of modern physics. Three of them were on Brownian motion, relativity and matter-

energy equivalence. The fourth paper is what won him the Nobel Prize (and not the third as people usually believe). Who was the author of these papers and what was the fourth paper about?

17. A study that researched the physics behind a seemingly superhuman person came up with these findings. His thin, long torso offers low drag. His arms span 6 feet 7 inches, which is unusually disproportionate to his height of 6 feet 4 inches, and they act as long propulsive paddles. His relatively short legs lower drag and add the speed enhancement of a hydrofoil. His size-14 feet provide the effect of flippers. His hypermobile ankles can extend beyond the *pointe* of a ballet dancer enabling him to ship his feet. Who was this study done on?

18. In 200 BC, King Hieron II commissioned a Greek mathematician to design the Syracusia, a huge luxury ship cum naval warship. Since a ship of such monumental size would leak a considerable amount of water through the hull, the mathematician built this invention, which could remove the bilge water. Operated by hand, it could transfer water from a lower area to a higher area, and till today, it is used for the same purpose. What is the name of this invention, which is named after the mathematician?

19. Ooblek is a type of fluid which temporarily gains the structural properties of solids when a force is applied on it. It does not have constant viscosity independent

of stress. Fluids that do so are referred to as 'X-ian fluid' after the name of a famous physicist. Ooblek is a non X-ian fluid and can be obtained by mixing two cups of cornstarch with one cup of water. There are plenty of videos on YouTube that explore the amazing qualities of Ooblek. Who is the physicist after whom these liquids are named?

20. The Coriolis Effect is governed by a force that acts on objects that are in motion within a frame of reference that rotates with respect to an inertial frame. These effects are supposed to show clear visual differences in the way water moves, depending on the place it is in. One common myth is that water flushes down the toilet clockwise in the northern hemisphere and counter-clockwise in the southern hemisphere. This has been proved to be wrong, as the Coriolis Effect does not work on such minute-sized bodies. There is, however, a natural phenomenon whose rotation is very much dependent on the Coriolis Effect. What huge (and nowadays mostly devastating) natural phenomenon has a different rotation in different hemispheres thanks to the Coriolis Effect?

ANSWERS

1. Steady State Theory
2. That the sun and the moon are of almost the same size
3. Electromagnetism

4. A piece of bread dropped by a bird! While CERN admitted feathers and bread were found at the scene, their final statement claimed it was just an electrical malfunction

5. The wires had been chewed through by a beech marten, an animal from the weasel family

6. Hawking Radiation, after Stephen Hawking

7. Alessandro Volta; the Voltaic Pile (battery)

8. Henri Becquerel and Marie and Pierre Curie

9. He is the only person to have won two Nobel Prizes in Physics

10. Edwin Hubble, after whom the Hubble telescope is named

11. Antimatter

12. Inside the Voyager spacecraft

13. Michael Faraday

14. Friction and centrifugal force

15. Aurora Borealis and Aurora Australis

16. Albert Einstein, Photoelectric Effect

17. Multiple-medal winning Olympian, swimmer Michael Phelps

18. Archimedes Screw

19. Isaac Newton (Newtonian fluids)

20. Hurricanes or typhoons

8. PSURPRISING PSYCHOLOGY

1. In 2007, a newspaper carried out an interesting experiment to see how people perceive their environment and what effect context has on what we notice. A world-famous violinist, who had performed in the city's biggest hall just two days previously, dressed casually and performed with a violin in a subway station. He played for forty-five minutes, and only six people slowed down to pay any attention to him. The newspaper went on to publish a story about this, talking about how little attention people pay to their environment even though a lot of people assume that 'art' or 'genius' will immediately grab attention. Which newspaper was this that published this Pulitzer Prize-winning story, and who was the violinist?

2. In 1968, Jane Elliott, a schoolteacher in Iowa, came up with one of the most fascinating experiments to teach children about discrimination. Her all-white class was divided into blue-eyed and brown-eyed students, and she then said blue-eyed students were smarter.

This led to an immediate sense of superiority, over brown-eyed students. The next day she announced she'd made a mistake and brown-eyed students were smarter and the roles were reversed. By the end of the second day, all the students had experienced discrimination and were more than eager to make friends with each other. Elliott's experiment has been reproduced in multiple contexts with stunning results. But it all came about because of a tragic incident that had taken place that year, pushing her to teach children about discrimination and bigotry the very next day. What was this incident?

3. In 1964, a young woman called Kitty Genovese was murdered in New York. Although many people heard the ruckus and her cries for help, no one came out to help her, and the first call to the police went out almost forty-five minutes after she was first attacked. This shocking incident led psychologists to study why so many people failed to help (this happened outside a residential apartment). Subsequent experiments showed that the greater the number of people witnessing a particular event, the less likely they are to come forward and help. Various life-saving tips have been developed based on this—for example, people trained in CPR are told to automatically assign roles to people around them. What is the name given to this phenomenon, whereby people around don't rush to proffer help?

4. Many studies have shown that children need visible

role models to show them what is possible in the world. Former tennis player and current coach Judy Murray is a passionate advocate for giving greater visibility to women sportspersons in order to show young girls interested in sports that this is possible. This phenomenon was demonstrated in the 1990s when a certain TV show portrayed one of the earliest accomplished female protagonists, who was a doctor and worked in the FBI. This character is supposed to have inspired a significant increase in the number of women taking up careers in science, medicine and law-enforcement. What is this effect, named after the character's name on the show?

5. In 1904, X, a Russian physiologist, was awarded the Nobel Prize for his work on digestive secretions. However, weirdly enough, this is the last fact that would occur to most people hearing X's name. In the course of his research into salivation, X made one of the most influential discoveries in the world of psychology. Who is X and what 'response' is he associated with?

6. In a study conducted in the 1960s and '70s, a child would be left alone in a room with a certain delicious object in front of them. They were told that if the object was still there when the adult returned, they would get two of those objects to eat. A follow-up study showed that the children who waited for the adult to return performed better in many areas of their life! What

was the sweet and soft object used, which gave the experiment its name?

7. As the amount of information available to us increases, researchers have found that rather than exploring subjects in a more detailed manner, most individuals tend to favour information that supports what they already believe and ignore or disbelieve contradictory information. This is an important finding, as it may show how to help humans be more objective and also explains how people retain such strong 'for' and 'against' stances. What is the name given to this tendency to only accept information we agree with?

8. Anna O became a highly significant name in the twentieth century (even though it was not a real name!). She was the patient of an Austrian neurologist, Josef Breuer. Breuer discussed her case with a friend and student, recounting how her mental illness was related to a childhood traumatic incident with a dog. This discussion went on to inspire his friend to develop one of the most influential psychological movements of that century. Who was Breuer's friend?

9. Wilhelm Wundt is often credited with being the father of 'Psychology' as a modern, standalone field. Wundt and his students carried out a series of scientific experiments in his lab, to measure and describe the workings of the mind. Where is this lab, which may be regarded as the birthplace of modern psychology?

10. In the 1970s, a pair of researchers decided to carry out an experiment. They told a group of students at a theological seminary in Princeton that the latter would have to deliver a sermon on a certain character from the Bible. Just before they left to deliver the sermon, each student was told one of three things—that they were either late, early, or 'just on time'. The students then encountered a stranger on the ground, who seemed to need help. The observers noted that the maximum help came from participants who were told they were early, while only 10 per cent of those who thought they were late stopped by to help. What made this experiment more interesting was the subject of the sermon they were supposed to deliver! Who was this person in the Bible they were going to talk about, and why did the findings of this study seem so ironic?

ANSWERS

1. *The Washington Post*, Joshua Bell
2. The assassination of Martin Luther King Jr.
3. The Bystander Effect
4. The Scully Effect (Dana Scully in *The X-Files*)
5. Ivan Pavlov, the Pavlovian response or classical conditioning
6. Marshmallow, The Marshmallow Test
7. Confirmation bias

8. Sigmund Freud, father of Psychoanalysis
9. Leipzig, Germany
10. The Good Samaritan, who, in the Bible, is the only
    passerby to help a man on the road

9. WONDERFUL WOMEN IN SCIENCE

1. The daughter of the poet Lord Byron, this lady had an interest in Mathematics since childhood. Her mother encouraged her to study Maths and Logic, in part to supposedly prevent her from developing the insanity which plagued her father. Her tutor was the extraordinary Mary Somerville, who herself was the first female member of the Royal Astronomical Society. Mary introduced her to Charles Babbage, with whom she developed one of the earliest computers—for which she wrote the program. As of 2015, both their pictures are featured in all British passports. Who was this lady, who, when she died at the age of thirty-six, was the world's only computer programmer?

2. This lady was a research associate at King's College in London in 1951. Her doctoral degree was on the porosity of coal for fuel purposes. Her colleague Wilkins showed a particular X-ray diffraction photo (#51) of hers (without her permission) to a friend called

Watson, who instantly realized the implications. This moment led to three Nobel Prizes, none of which even mentioned her. Who is this woman and what important event in science did she help bring about?

3. Caroline Herschel was born in 1750 and trained to become a singer. She later realized that her passion was the sky. She and her brother William got absorbed in astronomy and recorded observations meticulously. They recorded 2,500 new nebulae and star clusters. This was the basis for the *New General Catalogue*, by which celestial bodies are named to this day. She alone discovered fourteen new nebulae, eight comets and 561 new stars. This prompted King George III to employ her. This was possibly the first instance of what in the world of science?

4. One of the first palaeontologists in England was a woman named Mary Anning. Along with her brother, she collected a lot of shells, fossils such as ammonites and belemnites from coastal regions in and around her hometown. The two of them made fossils a family business. At age twelve, she discovered the very first complete fossil of a dinosaur. Her work is said to have contributed to big changes in the way nineteenth century geologists thought about the history of the earth. Most of us have heard of a rather twisted reference to her early days of collecting and marketing on the beach, created by a P.J. McCartney in his book *Henry de la Benche*. What is the reference, which is

usually taught to school children to improve their pronunciation?

5. Lise Meitner was an Austrian-Swedish physicist who, in the 1930s, was one of the foremost nuclear scientists in Germany. Due to her Jewish ancestry, she was forced to flee Germany and settle in Switzerland. Her working partner from Germany kept her updated about their work on a certain element. She was the first to realize that it was undergoing nuclear fission; splitting in half and releasing some of its tremendous store of nuclear energy. This was published in 1939 and it helped pioneer research that led to the use of nuclear reactors to generate electricity. She was unjustly deprived of a Nobel Prize in 1944, but had element 109, 'Meitnerium', named after her. Which element did she work on that changed history?

6. Barbara McClintock was an American geneticist whose ground-breaking work led to some of the most important advancements in biotechnology, such as the mapping of the human genome and CRIPSR/Cas9 gene editing. She spent her life analyzing the humble corn plant and examined and described its individual chromosomes. She went on to postulate the existence of transposons or jumping genes, which are sequences of DNA that move between the genome, for which she was awarded the Nobel Prize in 1983. She was also the first to suggest that genes alter their activity in response to external factors. What is this

concept of genetics she suggested, that changed the way scientists look at DNA?

7. Dorothy Hodgkin was a British chemist whose photograph was put up in 10 Downing Street by her student Margaret Thatcher. She was an expert in X-ray crystallography techniques and mapped the structure of insulin after thirty-five years of work, which became a stepping stone in the improvement of treatment for diabetics. She was also responsible for determining the atomic structure of cholestrol and penicillin. In 1964, she became the first (and as of 2019, the only) British woman to win a Nobel prize for he work in determining the atomic structure of a particular compound called 'cobalamin'. It is an essential compound in metabolism in the human body. What is the common name for 'cobalamin'—which is an important topic of debate nowadays, as it has been proven that vegans do not get this in their diet?

8. 'Amazing' Grace Hopper was a rear admiral in the United States Navy and one of the first programmers of the Harvard super computers during World War II. Hopper envisioned machine-independent programming languages and helped develop a programming language called COBOL, which is still in use. On 9 September 1947, her associates discovered a moth that was stuck in the relay of the Mark II computer and was hampering its function. Though neither she nor her crew used a certain term to refer to this, it has

become associated with the legend behind the term. What 'first' is this supposed to be, and consequently what term did 'Amazing' Grace coin?

9. In 1963, this lady became only the fifth ever human in history to do a certain thing. She logged in seventy hours of work, in the process compiling more time than all four American men who had done the same before her combined. She was twenty-six years old at the time, a full decade younger than the youngest man who had gone before. In the late '90s, it was made public that before the event, she had even found a bug in the landing program, which would have led to disastrous consequences if she hadn't resolved it. She had told her parents she was going for a skydiving competition, and they learnt about the event only in the news. Who is this record-setting lady?

10. This lady just wanted to leave her war-torn home and was unable to afford university. She worked as a secretary and saved up enough money to get to Kenya, where she met renowned anthropologist Dr Louis Leakey. He loved her enthusiasm and took her along on his expeditions. Soon, she became one of the first humans ever to gain the trust of an animal and be able to observe their behaviour up close. She was able to prove that these animals were not vegetarian as previously thought, but used tools to capture small animals and eat them. In 1965, she defied the odds to earn a PhD, though she did not have a degree. Who

is this lady, and our increasing knowledge of which animal species is thanks to her?

11. Dr Indira Hinduja is an Indian gynaecologist and obstetrician. In 1986, she delivered the very first test-tube baby in India. She is also credited for developing an oocyte donation technique for menopausal and premature ovarian failure patients. In 1988, she was the first doctor in India to use a technique called Gamete Intra-Fallopian Transfer, where eggs are removed from the ovaries and placed in the fallopian tubes. This was the precursor to IVF. By what fitting acronym is this technique known, which Dr Hinduja popularized in India?

12. This woman chose to study Physics at university and was faculty at the Central Institute of Physical Chemistry of the Academy of Sciences in her country. She went on to earn a PhD in the subject, with her doctoral thesis being on Quantum Chemistry. However, despite being such a highly educated physicist, she is known today for her work in a completely unrelated field. She took an interest in this field during a monumental period in her country's history and in 1989, entered a world that she would become a leader in. Who is this highly accomplished woman scientist who was the first woman in her country to hold a certain post?

13. Eunice Foote wrote an article which was published in *The American Journal of Science and Arts* in September 1856. It was titled 'Circumstances affecting the heat

of the sun's rays' and in two pages perfectly predicted a revolution in climate science by experimentally demonstrating the effects of the sun on certain gases and theorizing how those gases would interact with Earth's atmosphere for the first time. Three years later, Irish physicist John Tyndall published similar results, but this time his work was widely accepted and is globally accepted as the foundation of climate science. What did Eunice Foote predict, which is now a global issue but was ignored at the time due to gender bias?

14. Margaret Hamilton was working with NASA and developed the software which allowed the computer to recognize error messages, ignore low-priority tasks and continue to guide two men in a historic event. On 20 July 1969, Hamilton made some critical decisions as the world held its breath and was able to guide the two men to their destination with just thirty seconds to spare. At the age of thirty-two, she had led a team to a historic occasion. She has also been credited with popularizing the term 'software engineering'. What iconic mission did she develop the software for?

15. Abbie E.C. Lathrop was an elementary teacher who later started a poultry business. After that failed, she moved on to rodents, which she bred for hobbyists and pet owners. She kept very detailed records of her breeding programmes which proved to be immensely useful in a certain field. Soon top universities and even the US government came to her to purchase her

product. She even went on to author ten articles in cancer research thanks to her work ethic. What product did Abbie produce, which the scientific community is indebted to her for?

16. Jocelyn Bell Burnell was a grad student at Cambridge University in 1967 when she detected a faint, repetitive signal that she called 'scruff'—a regular string of pulses, spaced apart by 1.33 seconds—on the giant telescope they had just built on campus. She soon discovered more such pulses but at different speeds in different parts of the sky. She eliminated all the obvious Earth-origin explanations and gave it the name LGM-1 which stood jokingly for 'Little Green Men'. Her discovery was published in a journal and soon other astronomers realized what she had discovered was a previously unimagined form of neutron star that spun rapidly and emitted gamma radiation. This brought about a huge new change to astrophysics. What was the name given to these dense stars found by Burnell?

17. In 1953, Marie Tharp was a young geologist who made a map that proved a certain controversial theory at that time. She had discovered a 10,000-mile-long Mid-Atlantic Ridge which showed that there were certain movements which went against what was the general school of thought at that time. Unfortunately, her map was dismissed as 'girl talk'. After many months her collaborator Bruce Heezen published the work and took credit for it, and it was a seismic shift in geology

at that time. The ridge proved right a certain theory but Marie Tharp was left in the background. What theory did Tharp prove?

18. Naomi Weisstein is a neuropsychologist who in the 1970s was also a women's activist and a Rock and roll musician. In both her music and her science she was united in one theme—'resistance to tyrannies of all kinds'. After becoming faculty at the University of Chicago she started the 'Chicago Women's Liberation Rock Band' where they sang about sexism and gender liberation. In 1968, she wrote an article titled 'Kinder, Küche, Kirche as Scientific Law: Psychology Constructs the Female' which talked about three things that defined the role of women as mothers, wives and moral nurturers. What do the three 'K's stand for in German?

19. In 1970, Irene Peden was on the way to becoming the first female principal investigator working at a notoriously difficult place to work. Before she could step on to the plane for the last leg of the journey her chances were hampered as another lady who was supposed to join her failed her physical. The rule then was that to go to this hostile place there should always be at least two women. Men could go alone, women couldn't. At the last minute Iren found a local librarian who was also a mountaineer and they were able to get to their destination. She studied the electrical properties of the ice sheets

there and determined how Very Low Frequencies propagated over long distances. She even has a range of cliffs named in her honour. In which desolate place did Irene work against all odds and make scientific progress?

20. The Protein Information Resource is a free online database containing more than 200,000 protein sequences. It allows molecular biologists all over the world to take an unknown protein, compare it to the thousands of other known proteins and determine the ways in which it is similar or different. Using this information one can deduce its evolutionary history. The origins of this massive database is a 1965 book called *Atlas of Protein Sequence and Structure* which was compiled by Margaret Dayhoff. She applied what was at that time cutting-edge computer technology to find solutions to biological questions. This is the start of a field which is now one of the fastest-growing and most vital in Biotechnology. What field did Dayhoff usher in?

21. Maryam Mirzakhani was an Iranian mathematician and professor at Stanford University who specialized in Teichmüller theory, hyperbolic geometry, ergodic theory, and symplectic geometry. In 2005, she was acknowledged as one of the top ten young minds who have pushed their fields in innovative directions. In 2014 (three years before we unfortunately lost her to breast cancer), she became the first and (as of 2019) the

only woman to be awarded one of the most prestigious awards in Mathematics. Which award is this which is presented by the International Mathematical Union and known as the Mathematician's Nobel Prize?

22. Mae C. Jemison was the first Afro-American woman to be admitted into the astronaut-training programme as well as the first Afro-American woman to travel into space. She entered Stanford University at the age of sixteen, where she studied chemical engineering and Afro-American Studies. She went on to complete her medical degree from Cornell University and had a choice to either become a professional dancer or a general practitioner, and she chose the latter. In 1992 she became the first Afro-American woman to travel to space when she served as mission specialist on the Space Shuttle Endeavour. In 2019, to celebrate the fiftieth anniversary of the moon landings, she launched the 'Skyfie' challenge—which was to take a selfie with the night sky. She is also the only actual astronaut to have appeared on highly popular TV science-fiction show about humans and aliens travelling through space. In which TV show did she fittingly appear?

23. Patricia Bath was an Afro-American inventor and ophthalmologist. She was the first woman member of the Jules Stein Eye Institute, the first woman to lead a postgraduate training programme in ophthalmology, and the first woman elected to the honorary staff of the UCLA Medical Center. She also founded the

American Institute for the Prevention of Blindness under the premise that eyesight should be viewed as a basic human right. In 1986, she became the first Afro-American woman to obtain a medical patent for her device the 'Laserphaco Probe'. Laserphaco stood for 'PHoto Ablative C_____ surgery'. The probe improved the use of lasers to quickly and nearly painlessly remove a certain eye condition. With this she was able to restore vision in people who had been unable to see for decades. What eye condition did Bath treat with her patent?

24. Rachel Carson was a marine biologist and bestselling author, most celebrated for her 1962 novel, *Silent Spring*. The book was met with stern opposition by chemical companies, but the conservationist themes of this book had an important impact on furthering the global environmentalist movement. The book led to two monumental achievements. One was the inspiration of a grass-roots environmental movement that eventually became the US Environmental Protection Agency. The other was the US-wide ban of a particularly dangerous pesticide, traces of which have been found even at the bottom of the Mariana Trench. Which now-feared pesticide was completely banned thanks to Carson's book?

25. Hedy Lamarr was an Austrian actress whose stunning screen presence made her a global star in the 1940s. Her greatest success was as Delilah in the 1949 classic

Samson and Delilah. Bored of acting, she became a prolific inventor, designing an improved traffic stoplight and a tablet that, when dissolved in water, becomes a carbonated drink. She even designed bird- and fish-based wing designs for Howard Hughes' aircrafts. One day, while talking to composer George Antheil, they discovered a common passion for engineering and radiography. They went on to invent a 'frequency-hopping system' for use by the Allied Forces. What modern-day technology, that we often find ourselves the password for, came about because of the fantastic work done by this amazing lady?

26. Hertha Ayrton studied Mathematics, and during her study at Cambridge she constructed a sphygmomanometer and formed a Mathematics club. When she graduated in 1880, she did not get an academic degree because, at the time, Cambridge University gave only certificates and not full degrees to women. In 1884, she patented an engineering drawing instrument for dividing a line into any number of equal parts and for enlarging and reducing figures. Eventually, she went on to have twenty-six patents in her name. In 1899, she became the first woman ever to read her own paper before the Institution of Electrical Engineers (IEE). She was then petitioned to present a paper before 'X', which is the oldest national scientific institution in the world, but was not allowed because of her sex. She later was the first woman to be

nominated to the same, at a time when women could not be elected. Which institution was this that would not take her in?

27. Fabiola Gianotti is an Italian particle physicist who became interested in scientific research after reading a biography of Marie Curie. She went on to earn a PhD in experimental particle physics in 1989. On 4 July 2012 it was she who announced to the world that the elusive Higgs Boson had been discovered by her team. In 2016, she became the first woman director-general of a research organization that operates the largest particle physics laboratory in the world. What is the name of the organization that Gianotti heads, which physically spans two countries?

28. Kamala Sohonie was a biochemist who became the first woman in India to be granted a PhD in a scientific discipline. She researched the nutritive values of pulses, paddy, and groups of food items consumed by some of the poorest sections of the Indian population. When she first applied at this prestigious institution for a research fellowship, the then director, Nobel Laureate C.V. Raman, refused, saying that women were not competent enough to pursue research. After she held a satyagraha outside his office, he finally relented, but put down strict conditions—which, though she was insulted, she accepted. This paved the way for many more women to be admitted. At which institution was Dr Kamala

Sohonie the very first woman researcher?

29. Vera Rubin is an American astronomer who was the sole undergraduate in astronomy at Vassar College. She went on to prove the existence of galactic superclusters. Her biggest contribution to astronomy was when she uncovered the discrepancy between the predicted angular motion of galaxies and the observed motion, by studying galactic rotation curves. The outcome, known as the 'Galaxy Rotation Problem', became the evidence for the existence of a mysterious entity that astrophysicists believe make up almost 85 per cent of the entire universe. What did Vera Rubin provide evidence for, which has become one of the most studied entities in physics and also a very popular trope in science fiction?

30. 'X' is a charter established in 2005 and managed by the UK Equality Challenge Unit that recognizes and celebrates good practices in higher education and research institutions towards the advancement of gender equality. It also bestows awards to institutions which advance careers of women in science, technology, engineering, mathematics, and medicine (STEMM). The name of the charter has two words. The first word is the name of the Greek goddess of wisdom, who was associated with the capital city of Greece. The second word is an abbreviation of 'Scientific Women's Academic Network'. What two-word title does this charter have?

ANSWERS

1. Countess Ada Lovelace
2. Rosalind Franklin
3. First woman to be paid for scientific work
4. She sells sea shells, on the sea shore
5. Uranium
6. Epigenetics
7. Vitamin B12
8. Computer 'bug', debugging
9. Valentina Tereshkova
10. Jane Goodall, Chimpanzees
11. GIFT
12. Angela Merkel, first Female Chancellor of Germany
13. Global warming
14. Apollo 11 mission to the Moon
15. Lab mice for experimental purposes
16. Pulsars
17. Plate Tectonics
18. Kinder (Children), Küche (Kitchen), Kirche (Church)
19. Antarctica
20. Bioinformatics
21. Fields Medal
22. *Star Trek*
23. Cataract
24. Dichlorodiphenyltrichloroethane (DDT)
25. WiFi
26. Royal Society

ACKNOWLEDGEMENTS

I'd like to thank my bookshelves in Madurai and Bengaluru for bearing the weight of innumerable books, an absolute treasure trove of trivia. I'd like to thank all my teachers from Vikaasa School, Madurai, and The American College, Madurai, who have been instrumental in shaping me into this really annoying person who keeps questioning things and noting down random facts. To every science communicator who instilled in me the desire to seek information—Carl Sagan, David Attenborough, Neil DeGrasse Tyson, Brian Cox, Richard Dawkins, Bill Nye, Dana Scully—thank you for your work. It is only fitting that this book be dedicated to my house, 'Sharon', in Madurai, where my grandparents and parents raised me. Special thanks to my dad Ashley Rathinaprakash, who is even known as a 'mad scientist' by many, for surrounding me with two things that run my life—science and music. If it weren't for him, his soldering irons, kilometres of cables, tons of screws and piles of mechanical devices, I might have never known the joy of manually doing science.

Berty Ashley

I'd like to thank my family and my school (B.A.S.S, Kalakshetra) for encouraging me to read widely and ask questions and figure out how things worked. From early books on science and *How Things Work* that my parents read to me, to passionate science teachers in school, I came across a wide variety of information and facts—and as the years went by all the different facts I learnt came together.

In addition to these resources, both my grandmothers taught me to take a practical interest in how objects around us worked and how to set them right!

And lastly, I'd like to thank Berty for rekindling my interest in science and technology through the incredible and life-saving work he and Dystrophy Annihilation Research Trust are carrying out.

Akhila Phadnis